INFODEMIC

www.blacklawrence.com

Executive Editor: Diane Goettel
Cover Design: Zoe Norvell
Cover Art: "November's Raining Light" by Todd Horton
Book Design: Amy Freels

Copyright © Carol Guess 2024
ISBN: 978-1-62557-077-2

Published 2024 by Black Lawrence Press.
Printed in the United States.

INFODEMIC

CAROL GUESS

Contents

1978

My mother stood in Miami sun
behind the palm tree that grew two trunks.

My sister and I climbed in unison,
fronds' thick skin between us.

The car that stopped kept running.
Two men stepped out, arms stretched

to take us. I remember my mother
appearing so fast. I serrated my ankles

on sawgrass, drank piña colada
mix from the box. Candy canes

melted on the Christmas tree.
My father brought home a skeleton.

Showed me how surgeons suture.
His southern accent rose and fell,

phone cord stretched across the kitchen.
We colored computer cards on linoleum,

watched TV in black and white
while Jonestown broke, peeling

foil from frozen dinners. In roller skates,
under the disco ball, I danced

the Bus Stop with the all-skate line.
I believed I would survive.

*

Sunflower

Shake me and little teeth fall out. Birds beak my skin to scars. I wanted to send you a card a few years ago, but we didn't know each other then. Also I was a cat, but that was only temporary. At my worst I was an improperly installed electric stove that kept tipping over and eventually caught fire. Today I'm a sunflower. Today I'm beaming at you through the window. You can see me on the lawn, past the carport, if you squint.

The Year I Stayed Inside

Even the mirror asked too much.
Twisted, I cut
my ponytail in half.
Fur fringed the sink.
No one should watch
this much TV.
I knew the names
of the minor characters
in the fantasy suite.
So many ways
for straight people
to marry: meet cute,
meet unseen behind a wall.
On Twitter, blue checkmarks
subtweeted each other.
Everyone laughed when kids
burst in on men.
Sometimes I brushed
my top teeth twice.
My neighbor smoked
two packs a day, smoke
seeping through outlets
as I sat on my couch,
free trade chocolate
wrapped in gold.
WTF WFH
I was alone
with thoughts of what
I'd never say.
Mass shootings slowed

until the shots
met skin.
I bared my arm.
I wanted pain
to make TV less real.
In a gym, six feet apart,
we waited for bodies
to go into shock.
Some people left
before their time was up.

Unexpected Side Effects of the Second Dose of the Moderna Vaccine

Sometimes you turn into a crow.
You know the deal with flying now.

Money appears in your bank account,
but you're a fox and don't bank online.

Your arm swells big as a basketball
because you're a basketball.

Sometimes you turn to salt
until someone shakes you.

You're a snake. You're flames
licking the fireplace. You're summer

frogs hidden in the green becoming.
Sunlight falls across a room

where you hold out your arm,
where a needle teaches your body

how to fight back. You're unnamed
mice infected with the virus in a lab.

You're hands that feed the unnamed mice
just long enough to make the kill.

Thank You to the Needle for Not Wasting My Time

After, I sat with strangers
waiting for one to flail, for the needle to fail us,

a throat to close its singing pipe.
For breath to say *I'm outta here* and shut.

No one moved. We all left whole.
It takes three weeks and then two more.

My arm still itches, blushes in ripples.
We're talking 94%.

Always room for error. Always another room
where sickness waits to make us stranger.

Glory

My best friend told me about fucking this guy at the start of lockdown.
They'd been fucking for years, once or twice a month. This was body,
body, body. Anyway she went over to his place and stood outside in
her mask and he came outside in his mask and unlocked the garage.
They stood six feet apart. He lifted the door. Inside he'd set up a bed
bifurcated by a plastic sheet hanging from the ceiling. She looked at
him and nodded consent. He nodded back. They closed the door.

The Day My Best Friend Had a Pregnancy Scare

I wasn't scared
texting
6 in the morning
I told her I'd raise the baby
with her and that dude
whose name I couldn't remember
still can't white dude bearded
lives nearby she took
the test at lunch
peed on a stick
between swabbing noses
testing for Covid
110 noses a day
I said let's go live in the woods
somewhere maybe Canada
moose and geese
live that Canadian life
he can come too she said okay
I knew she was serious
because she used the emoji
she uses when she means
what she says sometimes
we're hyperbolic
she knew I wasn't
kidding I meant
let's go to the woods
let's raise a bébé
the only part I didn't mean
was him he could get lost
and I would not be sad

he never knew she thought
she was pregnant she never
told him only fucked
him it was me she loved
the stick said no baby
I hopped on a Zoom

The Year My Therapist Wore a Capsule Wardrobe

I was in love, but
The pieces fit
in layers,
never primary colors.
over another
tied twice around that.
hid a hole
She said follow
in a line.
shouldn't occur
Unraveling starts
thread. The scar
I was unreachable

not with her.
over each other
black and white,
I was something
and then a thing
The belt
that held in a feeling.
the dot as it moves
The hemstitch
to the eye.
with a single
a seam reveals.
for many years.

Next Time You See Me

thorns in my hair I don't wear shoes
anymore *how are you* leads
through switchbacks and scree
my dogs and I go everywhere
a grubby pack we sniff
rabbits leap-snap bees
my mouth has been covered all year
sit with me while I tell you
in silence how it was

Reentry

It takes a while to realize no one's watching.
You paint the gray wall white.
You give away your earrings
and the holes stitch shut.
Someone posts pictures
of missiles striking civilians.
Someone posts pictures
of their first meal unmasked.
You carry your laundry,
so many sleeves dangling.
One by one you slip your arms inside.

CDC Guidelines for Midafternoon

wow what a gif
breathing in public
sting of my teeth
gnashing hot air
do birds sense humans
making a comeback
reopening traffic
reloading guns
this morning a hawk
divebombed my dog
I carried her home
pressed to my chest
wasn't it something
the bright world without us
hitting refresh
birds live tweeting sky

There is No Goddamn Chip in the Vaccine

But if there was, maybe you'd like it.
Maybe you'd follow the voices

downtown. Break into the theater,
marquee blank for over a year.

All that popcorn, vats of fake butter.
Front row seats to four films on repeat.

You'd be an audience of one, hands cold
from the fountain drink of your choice.

*

Today I'm Trying

The dogs crush me on the couch. Everything I've ever done wrong
replays, streaming service I pay too much for. Sun through the window
becomes light through my fingers covering my face. No falling: not
sleep, not love, not off this couch. Look, I'm depositing a check without
moving anything but thumbs. Look at this money I earned working
year in, year out. There were doctors' appointments, teeth cleanings.
I remember restaurants. I remember driving to work, parking my car,
climbing the hill and thinking the car would always be there, a clunky
house carrying me away from home. Every day the lessons I learned
from quarantine slip into memories everyone made for themselves
alone. My mother's tumor wants to take over. Worms its way into her
skull. I've been having headaches for months: thin line connecting
us, unbreakable. This pain, that joy. I want to wrap her tumor around
my wrist, snap it, and break it. I want to eat it. Today, another mass
shooting in a food court at a mall. A shooter shot the shooter. Bennifer
got married and look, we have perfect weather here in my town. I can
see the mountains from my window when I'm washing dishes. The
water's too hot before I suds up and cool off.

Quiet Quitting

Yesterday I got rear-ended. Just now my key fob wouldn't work,
couldn't get back into the building. I was outside stuffing garbage into
the dumpster, crows divebombing a pizza-soaked sofa. Some dude
was pacing around recycling, talking to Dave, the building manager.
We followed each other out front, where our key fobs didn't work,
either. Dave this, Dave that. Yesterday someone died on the sidewalk
of the abandoned building next door. One light goes on upstairs at
night, facing my window but shielded by trees. It creeps me out, except
they're probably creeped out by me, white lady prancing around her
apartment all night with a key fob that never seems to work. My
sadness is definitely about the dead bodies. Seattle has a plan and its
plan is Let Our People Die. L tells me they're sleeping. Not everyone
on the sidewalk is dead, Carol. Actually, the sadness is about the key
fob in a roundabout way which connects back to my girlfriend, but I
don't feel like explaining. In some poems, the you is romantic. In this
poem, it's not, which is the problem I've always had with gender. It isn't
that I'm neither, it's that I'm good at both. I'm opposites so they cancel
each other out. Lately this means black nail polish, femme in a different
guise and I can walk right in. Like when the light goes green and
clicks and the door just opens. Like when you're in bed with someone
and touch them with little cat claws, bruises, like my blue, blue heart.
My best friend texts to say she's been quiet quitting since 1994. How
about loud quitting. How about employer-paid dental care that covers
cleanings. There's a line between staying open to change and pushing
your lover to be someone else. My girlfriend tells me she doesn't hate my
body just because she hates her own. Pinching her stomach: I just want
to be smaller. As small as what? A key, a bruise, shoes on the sidewalk
where they found the body.

Magnolia

With my window open, I smell railcars stopped on the tracks. There's half an airplane wrapped in green fabric. Trains and planes come here to die. I lived on the other side of the water a few years ago. Someone was sleeping in the dumpster behind my building. We were worried he'd fall asleep and be crushed in the compacter. When two guys crashed their car into our door, one of my neighbors ran down four flights of stairs and chased them around the block. He lost them on 15th, a street familiar with loss, with the chase, with dreams that end crumpled, hood crushed against stucco. We called it Phinney Gulch. I don't know what this neighborhood is called, or if it is one. Technically Magnolia, actually Interbay, so maybe MagBay or InterMag. MagInter and InterOlia don't really work. When I take walks I go up Dravus and over the hill, then down a flight of stairs that's only slightly creepy. More downhill, uphill again. The backend of Magnolia smells like white collar crime. There are no encampments. No one living in RVs or tents. No one sleeping in doorways, urinating in the alley. No one picking food out of a dumpster, fighting with crows for a handful of French fries. There's no garbage on the lawns or sidewalks. No dog shit. Nothing out of place. Long streets of leisure. There's one grocery store on the backend and literally every item is five dollars more than it should be. Sometimes I walk my dog through the tree-lined streets, looking out at the Sound, smelling lavender. The idea of whiteness makes this neighborhood possible. There's almost no political signage, but as I walk down the hill there are a few scattered rainbow flags, a few BLM signs. One Real Rent Duwamish sign in the whole neighborhood. Then I'm on my street, which faces the tracks behind a row of trees filled with raccoons so bold they watched me unload when I moved in. Six raccoons beneath the pines, just watching. Calling me out as the stranger I am.

That's Not Pole Dancing

L's taking pole dancing as part of aging-in-place. Like cabinets behind
cabinets, wider doors, polished hardwood, glittering light fixtures,
new bathroom, new kitchen, new car. I'm trying to picture L on a
pole, thighs gripping while she arches back. I can't. This is a failure of
my imagination. L describes the class: we sit and stretch, we hold onto
the pole and arch our backs up and down like cats. L, that's ballet.
No, she says, the pole is vertical. What kind of music do they play?
She says classical. I'm exhausted at the start of every day, more Trump
this, Trump that, MAGA in every chyron. The fascist machine builds
power. Even antifa mispronounces antifa. My therapist and I talk about
The Bachelorette, which has a dual bachelorette season going. The two
contestants seem gay to me. They hug and smoosh boobs and say they
love love love each other. They say you are more important than any
man. It's pole dancing, L says, like she's going to cry. I've pushed her too
hard, like I push away cishet men in hot yoga trying to get my number
so they can talk about what. What would we even talk about. Tell me
one thing. This is the point of the show: get the women to shut up and
hold flowers. I want L to say that she's wrong, but she won't, like she
won't admit she's lonely since her wife died. She's not in love with that
woman in Bremerton. We promise to walk our dogs together, which we
both know will never happen. L has a house with a yard in Magnolia.
Every cabinet has a cabinet hidden behind it, but when I ask her what's
hidden, what secretssextoysdrugsdelights, she says nothing. She says it's
good to have extra storage. She says her favorite part of the class is when
they lie down at the end and pretend that they're dead.

Hardware Store Birds

None of the new keys work. They're making them off the wrong blank
key, an endless supply of ways to be stuck. The hardware store birds stay
caged in back, not even a window. They stare all day at the key making
machine that's doing the wrong thing. The neon pig knows what BBQ
means. Smiling chicken offering her body to be burned alive, breaded and
fried. The vacant lot beside my building shimmers with wildflowers and
staycation gulls. Someone's parked their boat under wrinkled gray tarp.

Blue

You're in her DMs but I'm locked out of her building. By her building,
I mean mine. You're the beanstalk and the talking horse. You're the
candy house and I'm the oven. Today my best friend and I had coffee
in a shop midtown. Both phones on, face down on the table. She said
cupcake. I said cupcake. Now it's cupcake, cupcake on every ad. You're
representing yourself in court. You're taking notes but I'm already
taken. The key fobs to my building still don't work, so the door's
propped open with Everyday Blue. These chewable vitamins taste too
good. I shazam my old dog's snores. The app spins its lightning logo. It
doesn't recognize the song.

Highly Classified

While I was vacuuming, I discovered classified documents. Some of the documents included information about nuclear weapons and some of the documents included names of secret agents.

Attached to one of the documents was a note with a phone number: PLS CALL IF LOST

"How may I help you?" the automated voice asked.

"I found classified documents under my bed."

"Take the classified documents and put them in a bag."

I put the documents in a tote bag that said READING IS SEXY.

"Put the bag in the garage."

"I don't have a garage. I live in an apartment."

"Put the bag in the garage."

"I don't even have a street parking permit."

I went outside with the bag over my shoulder. The automated voice continued talking to me through my ear buds. I walked until I got to the part of my city where there were houses with garages, but none of the garage doors were open.

I sat down inside a bus shelter to think. The bus shelter was nice because the neighborhood was nice. There was no graffiti. The bus shelter had a clean bench and a trash can lined with a bag. There was a sign on the trash can that said, "No dog waste." The entire neighborhood had signs saying, "No dog waste," images of dogs pooping with tiny turds coming out of their butts. Most of the houses in this neighborhood were several stories tall, modern, wood and sometimes metal. They towered over the bungalows they'd mostly replaced. The numbers on the houses were all designed in the same style. A few had Astroturf in the front lawn. Their garages were locked, and they had Ring cameras installed in their doorbells.

A bus pulled up to the shelter. I waved my bus pass and climbed on. With my earbuds in, I scrolled through TikTok. I made a TikTok on the bus in which I played the latest music and joked about carrying highly classified documents in a tote bag that said READING IS SEXY. While I rode the bus aimlessly, my follower count kept climbing. My TikTok went viral. Soon people getting on the bus recognized me. "You're the TikTok artist," they said. "You're the one carrying the nuclear codes in a tote bag."

Before I could decide which stop to exit, I had offers from several companies to create content around my hilarious classified documents joke. "Ha ha," they said, "so funny." I signed with a fast food company to do a commercial where I reached into my tote bag and pulled out a hamburger, only it was a vegan burger, so the ad was cosponsored by a plant-based meat company. I also signed to do an ad for an underwear company where I reached into my tote bag and pulled out gender-neutral underwear, smiled at the camera, and said, "Underwear is sexy!" I also auditioned for Saturday Night Live but didn't get it.

When the bus pulled into the city lot after midnight, the driver told me it was the last stop, and I'd have to get off. As I hopped off the bus, I realized we were in a garage. I looked at the driver and he looked at me. He nodded, and I handed him the bag.

The Mar-a-Lago Pool Tech Speaks

Don't come at me, guns blazing. That shit scares me. I don't care which
side you're on; you're not on mine. Do you know the cost of bread,
weight of coins in your pocket instead of paper? Placket on a work
shirt, logo on the collar. I've got a wife at home, a kid whose legs and
teeth need braces. My job's filtration. I rescue drowned leaves from the
chemical blue. The back of my neck burns red. You think you know
which way I ride. But Florida fixes its mistakes. Stare at the sky for
hours, never see the same blue twice. Order death by alligator, traceless,
pure disappearance. Bury your ex on the links, casket too heavy for a
body. Anything's possible. Surveillance is only as good as rewind: that
fat red button. I swim laps in the off-season dark, lizards flickering
against the lime green screen. Sawgrass cuts just like a blade. My hands
are clean.

Ketchup on the Wall

I'm not even a vegetable. All I know to be is red. Ripeness becomes me, same after same in a field intertwined, vines prickling. I swore an oath to sun and grew. How did I go from globe to lob, from blood red skin to tattered seed strings? A stain, a punchline. Smeared. I was meant for a mouth, but now I'm trashed.

Trump on the Links

WTAF
he still plays golf
free man
on the green
white shirt
no cuffs

American Carnage

Do you remember
when Trump told us
to inject bleach
into our veins
to cure us
of the deadly virus?
We wanted to be clean.
Bleach whitens things.
We collect nicknames
for Covid-19: covies,
rona, pancetta, panini,
panic button, pied-à-terre.
We're dying and we're still
so fucking funny.
We stayed inside,
paid someone else
to deliver our groceries.

*

The Devil Found Me

the devil found me
god never did
in the backseat
of a car in a train
station in the Olympic
National Forest holding
a mirror under my skirt
this is why I don't believe
in god I know
who to run from
that should be
enough

Swerve

Someone I love
someone I always
will love
swerves
in certain conversations
suppose a woman
stays out late
sits alone at a bar
suppose she's harmed
subtle at first
words become worry
for the person who harmed her
is he okay
he might be hungry
might not get a job
might sit alone
when he goes to the bar

The Moment I Heard the Twig Snap Behind Us

wasn't the moment I knew. By then we'd filled our pockets
with rocks, picked up sharp branches, hiked deep in the forest

dizzy with switchbacks. I knew from the beginning, at the trailhead
when I saw the car's dead-eyed driver. You knew, too.

We forgot what we knew because knowing felt dangerous.
This is how I relearn the lesson: not knowing is worse.

I knew that, too, as I knew on instinct how to flag
down a truck without knowing the driver.

I hopped into the bed beside you, reciting the license.
The stranger who'd chased us for miles

through switchbacks stood at the trailhead
inhaling exhaust. Panting in the bitterbrush.

White Truck

We took the dogs to the easy hiking trail. Not a hike but a walk. Not a walk but benches and trees. You could sit. You could sing, although the birds were quiet. Were there any birds out there that day. The white truck parked at the entrance was still parked when we returned from slow circles with the heartbreak dogs. There was a machete on the bumper of the truck. You picked it up.

"Should I take it?" you asked, not really asking.

But I didn't want to ride with you if you were holding a knife, if you had something so silver almost inside you.

I already knew too much, even though I knew nothing.

Were the birds really singing or did I cry out. Was I silver nothing in the bed of your truck. Was I the one who saw the blade.

You drove home with one hand on the wheel, one hand well-played.

Complicata

You took me out to a field. I mean a room. I mean a field with twin hawks circling. I mean a bed and bedside lantern. You took me and you took me, and all the roses made me sneeze.

I'm allergic, I said. To roses.

To roses?

The ways you didn't believe me and the ways you did. The way the porch light flickered as you rearranged thorns. I mean roses. I mean the roses made a sound when you cut their throats.

You handed me a bouquet and what could I do.

I pressed flowers in a book and gave the book to you.

Overdue

You live in Fool's Valley. You are the valley, and no one is fooled. You are the valley and I am your fool. You are the valley. I am a fool. You are the valley and I am the valley and together we curve, apostrophe S. The fool is long gone, and it wasn't his valley. It isn't ours, either. We're just white folks who live here.

I drove to Fool's Valley to see you, but you were already gone. I thought I knew where I'd find you and I was right. The other library, on the east side of town, hanging out with that librarian, Megan.

I said what are you doing with that librarian, Megan.

Nothing, you said. I read lots of books.

My Imposter

My Imposter goes out into the street and does not return. We had a fight; it's true. Days later I see them arm-in-arm with another Imposter. They look so happy, like they finally found their better half. They smile and wave and overshare.

"We're brilliant together," they say. "They understand me, because they're an Imposter, too. The sex is fantastic, because they know how everything works."

How can I compete with that?

I try to look happy for how happy they are. Then I invite them to lunch. They both say no, sorry, too busy, and besides, food allergies. They're allergic to me.

"But you live inside my head and eat what I eat," I say to the empty sidewalk. They're gone already. I'm talking to myself.

You Are a Danger Clown and I'm Done with You Forever

dude I don't want to take walks with you anymore you're flirting
with wrong people you have bad energy I don't want to be around
you anymore even though your hair cuts a clean crisp line
on the back of your neck and I know what your lips taste like
is it sad or magical that I smell you when I'm crying or truly happy
you ruined my life for one hundred years in lesbian time my dude
how many rivers do I have to swim I threw my ring over the bridge
on one side a tent on the other side a tent people living on either side
of the bridge how long before we live on the bridge how long before
we live underwater in Seattle people live beside the freeway
not even tents just tarps over clothesline sleeping beneath trees
piles of belongings mistaken for garbage deliberately swept away by police
what does it mean that we won't house our people where do city limits stop
why are we all falling apart at the same time sick with the same sickness
infecting each other desperate for money or love confusing the two
it's unbearable to live here meaning anywhere my dude
why are you still a jerk didn't tragedy change you it sure changed me
I'm not the same person I was I just want to live you want to make trouble
but trouble is already here guns poverty hopelessness white people
also I'm white people how do I reconcile that it's easier to stir
small messes of the heart than stand in the shallow water and pray

Conflict to Civility

You take the fox,
I'll take the bear.
Let's pour our dead
into a bowl
and split the ashes.
Just don't take
my father's ghost.
He's mine,
and I don't want him
to know we broke up.

Golden Hour

Dandelions under chin after chin, buttery gold shadows. I suck on stems and wish on fennel. Here's where I bury the past, furry and quadraphonic. No bubbles when I text, just white on blue on black. This last gold loves you back.

What Is A ~~Divorce~~ Poem?

A ~~divorce~~ stays with you like an echo.

A ~~divorce~~ conveys emotions, ideas, and/or stories through attention to both sound and sense.

A ~~divorce~~ allows for figurative, as well as literal, meaning.

A ~~divorce~~ invites imaginative leaps and playful gestures.

A ~~divorce~~ can and does mean many things at once and doesn't require its meaning to be pinned down.

A ~~divorce~~ doesn't need to be concerned with facts, but it does need to be honest.

A ~~divorce~~ doesn't need to rhyme. The music of the ~~divorce~~ should suit the mood of the ~~divorce~~. There is a different music for every ~~divorce~~.

A ~~divorce~~ doesn't need to tell a story or make sense, but it needs to have an impact on an audience wider than one. It can't be a personal expression of pain, or a personal joke or story, or so secretive that the audience is shut out entirely. A ~~divorce~~ is written to be shared, unlike a diary entry.

A ~~divorce~~ is allowed to be hard to understand only if the work the audience puts into it eventually pays off.

A ~~divorce~~ can be political but doesn't have to be.

A ~~divorce~~ can be autobiographical or fictional or both, but if it conveys the sense that it is somehow factually true in the context of factual truth that matters, then it should be factually true. For example, using statistics about how many people are currently incarcerated in America implies that those statistics are true. To invent them would be dishonest and do a disservice to others. But it's okay to have a dragon fly in and free the prisoners.

A ~~divorce~~ should sound distinctive because the voice is authentic, not because the voice is pretentious. It's okay to sound like you sound in real life. ~~Divorce~~ is real life.

A ~~divorce~~ makes people feel things—sad, happy, excited, calm, energized, angry, alive. It can be intended to provoke emotion, although it shouldn't be manipulative and sentimental.

A ~~divorce~~ situates others in the language world of a particular time and place. The language of the ~~divorce~~ should reflect and challenge contemporary language conventions.

A ~~divorce~~ doesn't give a lesson in life. A ~~divorce~~ isn't an instruction manual. A ~~divorce~~ doesn't tell you what to do or feel or think.

A ~~divorce~~ trusts that you will bring your own life experiences to the ~~divorce~~ and therefore every reading of a ~~divorce~~ is different.

A ~~divorce~~ invites rather than demands. If a ~~divorce~~ demands, the demand should be part of an overall aesthetic of protest or inspiration, but it must still be artistically skillful.

A ~~divorce~~ can work only on the page or only spoken aloud, but it's great if a ~~divorce~~ does both.

A ~~divorce~~ is original and reflects individual voices and values.

A ~~divorce~~ should be at least a little bit surprising.

Everyone creates bad ~~divorces~~ sometimes. Everyone is capable of a few great ~~divorces~~. The best ~~divorce~~ comes after many years, practicing and refining your skills. Everyone makes mistakes and it's okay to face rejection, craft some lousy ~~divorces~~, and keep trying. No one creates a perfect ~~divorce~~ immediately and even the best ~~divorces~~ still have to work hard.

If you want to make more ~~divorces~~ and revise them and keep making ~~divorces~~, eventually you might want to send your ~~divorces~~ out into the world and see if you can get them accepted. I suggest looking at ~~divorces~~ in magazines and reading more books about ~~divorce~~ to refine your understanding of what a ~~divorce~~ can do.

Welcome to the world of ~~divorce~~. You can stay here as long as you want.

TLDR

When I was born, they gave my mother a manual with detailed instructions. Because I'd absorbed my twin, eaten them alive, their heart bloomed inside me. Their heart was more compassionate, or so the manual said. My heart, the manual said, was broken.

When Britney sang, "Hit me baby one more time" on Instagram, she slowed it down, made a pop song into a dirge. She sang as someone betrayed, imprisoned.

They made a movie of my life. They knew the ending, but I asked them not to tell me. I had to leave the premiere of my own movie early, so I wouldn't find out when the music stops.

The Half-Century Sibling

three years a star
no sister no hair
mistaken for a boy
perhaps not wrong
when my hair showed up
my sister showed up too
red hair small sister
I was not pleased

missing the sister
I had missing
what was missing
between us
I troubled the twist
in my spine
into a twin

feral teeth
nipping
parasitic
kid twister

eighth grade
feminine hygiene spray
the other cheerleaders stuck
my head in a toilet

it's true I was queer

my parasitic twin
was never a bully
we hung out
at Lum's
eating key lime pie

Fundamentals of Appliance Repair

The refrigerator inside me breaks down, shudder and hiss, tiny foods sunning themselves at the beach of the broken refrigerator. The washer-dryer and dishwasher inside me keep working, glug-glug sass, powered by white soap pillows. All this inside me in the tiny kitchen. The tiny bedroom stays off limits. I have to hold something back now that I'm unmasked. The house inside me has cats, but who knows how many? I build a catio for the cats inside, set out kibble and catnip mice.

From the Freeway

The covered bridge sits wrapped in plastic, diverting traffic. What do birds think of this oblong egg? With your fingers in my mouth, I don't think anything at all. We have 10 dogs, maybe 12. Each dog carries a small ball of resentment. Never enough time to get ahead in this life. My toothpaste shines blue as the stoplight in a town that never got the memo. Look at the lake from the freeway, tinfoil smoothed over leftovers. I wanted to keep hearing voices, but the sign said stop.

Stray

Sunlit poppies, carnations, roses that prickle your throat until breathing stings. Birds singing an untranslatable song. The word *bird* all wrong, as if one bird was just like the others. The high-pitched sound you can't hear that sets the dog crying. How *dog* is also wrong. How your name never fit: the blandest name they knew. Their gift. There are a thousand ways to love and still be wrong about a name. This dog won't run to the name you call; too many names in too many shelters. She never comes, solves the problem in silence. Never leaves your side.

The Hour of Dog Park Drama

fur zooming
urination and delight
days after
vaccination
bite blooming
my arm red
sunset over
Westcrest Park
refusing to bide
temporarily wild
little dog spun
in the small dog lot
dust clouds kicked
by a five pound
chihuahua
Go Gizmo Go
herding six blurs

The Day the Dogs and I Broke the Field Behind Rows of Identical Pastel Houses

Light throttled
the bottleneck.

We climbed mud
up to the little dog's

chest. Hawks held circles
steadfast overhead.

I went looking
for a christening.

Will I ever
be clean again.

Why We Rush

Off kilter, we practice blur. Fur tufts fringe fallen needles. The forest
falters at the road. We're hop and habitat, instinct and sternum.
You're speeding and we want you to slow down, show us your tire eyes,
spinning wheels of scent from far flung furrows. Howling at sirens:
we're here. Dumpsters bloom cellophane and half-eaten heels. Trees
root for the hills.

Hidden So It Feels Like Mine

City park, half-finished, with a mundane name, hidden at the end of a cul-de-sac. Down the hill to the riverbed, dry stones, dead fish creviced where water ran out. Dog's fur prickles. He knows so much I'll never. I wait for the signal: forward or back? One twitch, and he's off running under canopy. We do this every day. It's the only thing I want to do, the only time I can forget to remember. My mother's cancelled her appointment on Wednesday. She doesn't want to know what's next or what's inside her. My life right now: stand under green and wait. Follow the prickle on the back of my neck.

Wins for Today

My mother sent me two blue potholders.

Opening the box, I smelled her perfume.

What If I'm Wrong

Footsteps after midnight, gray blur, that tilted feeling of hesitation. It isn't that the ghost is dead; it's that I'm still alive. Smoke off the burning mountain. Look at the flowers outside, trying to thirst trap their way through drought. Ghosts startle out of their kitchen, parallel to mine. The dog trots off, making room to haunt. When we meet again, I'll know it's time.

*

Ascent

This is a fairy tale: the handmaiden follows the princess, clutching the reins of her horse, counting trots to water, because water upends the social order.

Increasingly people move here for the water: to drink.

Did you know that if you marry someone and bring them coffee every morning and commit to having sex with only one person, you will both die?

My father died in his study. His cat died three days later. My mother cried about his cat but still can't cry about my father: some doors are best left shut.

The handmaiden escapes the castle in stealth. She's dragged to death by a team of horses.

I come from a long line of chicken farmers and blacksmiths in Sweden, where the cold drilled into our bones and stayed.

What I love about where I live now: a snowboarder's red pant leg in a tree well. Digging with a plastic shovel: "Are you okay, dude?"

In snow rescue videos, boarders and golden shepherds shake off frozen water.

We never see the other angle, the submerged camera, limbs becoming tree roots, subterranean griefwork.

Concussed

You share that you were once concussed.

You lay in the dark for months while your brain repaired itself,
rewiring. After, ghosts dressed in mothwings rustled the ceiling.

Friends encouraged you to lie about the accident: *On my bike, rounding
the last curve of the Tour de France! Lifting rubble to free a child trapped
in an earthquake!*

In truth you stood up too quickly in the chicken coop, forgetting how
tall you were, how short the chickens.

When we met, you'd only recently emerged from dim rooms in your
dim house, electronics off, not even the smoke alarm's red dot. The
doorway to the coop was stained with blood where you'd hit your head.

Because of your blood, the chickens were spared.

Best Practices for Weird Shit

You were wearing that shirt when you talked about dissection.

You had your hands in my body talking about a body, but we both knew which body you meant.

So many names for flowers but not the flowers on your shirt.

You unbuttoning.

You talking about dissection is a love poem.

We Keep Going Because We Can Never Turn Back

I want to unsee what I saw.

I didn't mean to make you see it.

In bed, looking up, filled with want, then startled.

At first I thought decoration. Then I thought lights on the ceiling. Stars that glow in the dark.

But not.

That wasn't what I saw.

I gasped.

You asked. I pointed up, and the sheet fell away from skin, tattoos, and scars.

"To the right of the ceiling sprinkler," I said.

Silence until you saw it.

I knew already that you weren't afraid of spiders. Earlier that night we'd watched a spider crawl across the floor. We both admired its span, its sense of purpose. It made its way behind your bookcase. None of the dogs chased it or ate it.

I said the word sad, an inadequate word.

"Its suffering is over," you said. It was the right thing to say.

I leaned into your shoulder.

The spider in the ceiling trapped forever under paint was not a symbol or an omen or a guide. It was a dead thing someone killed on accident or possibly on purpose. The white walls were painted before you moved in.

It didn't make sense to say more about suffering when suffering was all around us. When, driving home from the restaurant where we sat outside under brilliant red umbrellas, we'd passed tent after tent on the sidewalk. It didn't make sense to talk about death when death was already in the room.

It did mean more that you hadn't killed the spider earlier. Together we'd watched its leggy walk, admiring all it knew.

Zero Inbox

The fox in my chest spins
so I don't need a heart:
not heartless
but furred and fired up.
I'm glad I have a fox
and not a giraffe.
So much folding in half.
Reading my work email
I learned you were dead
which explained why
you hadn't texted.
This has nothing to do
with my eyebrows
so pale they're invisible
unless someone gets close.
I cast spells before I knew
what spells could do
to a body. I spelled
your name out loud.
I was afraid you'd find out.

Paradigm Shift Fatigue

today I tried to text you a smell
but you were dead
and the technology does not exist
I'll tell you a secret:
I don't like children
not even a little
I don't think they're cute
what no one talks about
is how hard it is
as an aging homosexual
to shift from hearing
I should not have kids
how if I had kids
they would be taken away
even close family
weird about kids   ·
then this window opened
where suddenly gay people
were supposed to want kids
were supposed to get married
it's like how I ordered
a white noise machine
from the behemoth corporation
ruining my city
the white noise machine
came in a box
which came in another box
and a box around that
I plugged it in
I turned the dial

Babbling Brook
Thunderstorm
Washer and Dryer
but every stop on the dial
was the same conversation
the last conversation
before you ended your life
what no one talks about
is how queer people survived
our oppressive childhoods
to keep your kids alive

Because I Could Not Stop

I found your body, but your body was birds. They flocked over your bed, you-shaped, cats sparring on the weighted blanket. When the police came, they said they found your body, but whose body was it?

Not the doughnut man.

Not the custodian killed in the latest mass shooting.

Not the Zumba teacher with hips smooth as cream.

I was trying to be vegan, like last year but different. When it snows here, the heart attack of sideswiped trucks convulses the city. It was a "wellness check," meaning they thought you were dead. When I twirled off tempo in my fourth grade recital, I lay down and played dead because that's how swans end.

Ghosted

My father's ghost ghosted me.

He disappeared when I invited you in.

I spoke to your ghost, meaning whatever you were now: dumplings, icicles, the message you didn't leave when you called and hung up.

"Hey," I said. "I know you were suffering. I know you couldn't hold on any longer. The dogs are here on your spot on the sofa. Don't be lonely. Come hang out."

The second I finished speaking, glass shattered and didn't stop. It sounded like all the windows in all of the apartments breaking at once, everyone throwing plates and cups. The sound came from outside my window. I got up and looked, but there was nothing unusual.

"Never mind. It's okay if you have other people to see."

Immediately the shattering stopped, replaced by static.

I called out to my father's ghost the way I do when anything troubles me, reaching for him in my mind. He was still there after his death, a little different maybe, but always with me.

Now he was just gone.

You weren't here, either.

My apartment was silent. The dogs' fur stood up in ridges.

Replacement Ghost

My father's ghost never came back. Instead Tony showed up, reeking singed oil from the garage fire that did him in.

"It was arson," he said, burping. Tony wasn't my ghost and I wasn't his person. He just ended up here and decided to stay.

Sometimes we talked about ghost things and sometimes we talked about people things. He always sat on the same side of the sofa. My side. Sometimes it was nice having company, but then I thought about how protective my father's ghost was.

"Can a ghost murder another ghost?" I had to ask.

Tony sunk a little deeper into the sofa. "I don't think so."

"You're lying."

"Don't I make dinner for you, even though I can't eat? Don't I pick up dog poop in the yard, even though I don't have hands or a body?"

It was true. Also, I missed your ghost, but your ghost had pushed my father's ghost out first. I tried asking Tony about you, but he got embarrassed.

"What is love?" his voice softened. "What does it mean to be close to another person? Can we ever really know them or is it all a façade?"

When I went to work the next day, I left him the book my therapist told me about. It was a self-help book about attachment theory. When I got home, Tony was in the kitchen, crying.

"I'm disorganized and dismissive and avoidant and anxious all at the same time. And I set the fire myself, for the insurance money, but look at me now."

I looked at him now. He was invisible but I could feel his energy and smell the oil, which hung from him in the shape of a person, or maybe a wrench. This was when I knew he'd leave, and the house would go back to smelling like peanut butter.

"Are my ghosts ever coming home?"

Tony's singed oil crackled.

Bread

My replacement ghost Tony asked for a spousal hire.

"Ghosts don't get spousal hires."

"Sure they do. I get a spousal hire or a personal shopper. Which one do you want to live with?"

It was all too much. Tony "accidentally" dumped my B-12 capsules and Easily Digestible Fruit-Flavored Iron gummies into the compost. Tony left sticky notes all over the house, with spoilers for "Love is Blind." Tony played "Say My Name" on repeat whenever I asked Siri for directions.

"Do I have any say in this at all?"

"No."

The next morning when I woke up, the house smelled like freshly-baked bread, homemade in the oven which I never used. I helped the old dog downstairs, following the smell. Tony was asleep on the couch, snoring.

That was when I noticed a new ghost in the kitchen. She was washing the dishes I'd left in the sink, the dishes Tony was supposed to take care of.

"Hey. I'm Monica."

"Are you Tony's spousal hire?"

"No, I'm his personal shopper."

I pulled out a stool from under the counter. Monica sat next to me, shimmering.

"It's okay. You can ask questions."

"What do you shop for?"

"I was kidding about all that. They put ghosts in pairs. Tony just got here early."

"Were you and Tony married?"

"God no." She laughed. "I've never seen him before in my life."

A UPS truck rumbled past the door and the dogs barked until it was gone.

"Do you know what happened to my ghosts? I mean the people I loved who died."

"Sorry. They don't tell us anything important."

She was easy to talk to. We sat for a while longer, not talking.

"Is there actually bread in the oven?"

"That's just how you'll know it's me."

Wreath

Your ghost came back, arms full of roses.

What type of ghost leaves and comes back?

What type of ghost will I be, hellhound?

I mean spellbound.

I mean you meant well.

I mean my name in someone's mouth.

You asked for a ring, but you meant a ring camera.

You owned nothing, not even yourself, because you weren't a self, just salt I dreamed up when I forgot you were dead and talked to you like you might answer or started to text you and stopped myself after two letters.

You wanted a ring for its eye.

You wanted to watch me watching, pretending I was you watching me.

Personal safety, all that.

I never cried for you or my father, but I cried about the camera's eye, cold and looking always one way at the street, which was a "private lane," meaning narrow and riddled with potholes, dog shit the neighbors never picked up.

That eye.

I watched it staring.

You called me *charming*.

Crown Shyness

I almost forgot to die today. When the reminder popped up on my phone I was in a meeting. "Sorry, I have to take this," I said, stepping out.

*

Today's death wasn't memorable. Today I died, etc., like I always do. Then went on living. Look at the sticky notes all over my desk. Such a mess.

*

Look, Death, you're wearing me out. You showed up at that party and spilled your drink on me. You flirted with me and we made out, but did we need to do it in the bathtub of the only bathroom at the party, people crammed into the kitchen, all needing to pee, desperate while we stuck our tongues in each other's dirty mouths?

Also, you've got me all wrong. I'm a homebody type, ink stains on my whorls. I make up worlds. Death, I didn't make you up, but I waited for you to follow me into the bathroom.

*

Today I died in your arms. While we were eating noodles on your sofa I turned to you and said, "It's time for me to die."

You laughed.

"I'm serious." Color draining from my face, nails blushing pink to polar blue.

"C'mere," pulling me into your chest. I felt happy and almost apologized for the impact my impending death would have on every subsequent relationship, but my breath was so slow, Death, stalled in my throat.

*

I stopped looking at the calendar. There was a page with a number. That was the day you died. After that, the numbers went backwards, traveled back to before you were dead, so you were still alive. I was also alive in this calendar whose numbers ran backwards. We were both alive until we weren't yet born. When we weren't yet born, we took turns spinning the globe.

*

Before the safety and wellness check, I found your body. Your boss was on the phone with the police, setting things in motion. Things that could not be undone. I guessed that you kept a spare key on the second sill and look: your cats were out of water. Drinking from the toilet bowl. I found your body first. You were in bed, half under your green weighted blanket. Your body lifted up and flew. Don't we all become birds in the end, I remember saying, but not to you, arms full of flowers, decomposing.

*

We sat on your sofa and watched the screen saver. You didn't want to commit to a movie. We watched aerial footage of the Snoqualmie National Forest.

That was when I knew. First I knew we'd never watch movies, only your screensaver; also, I knew you wanted to die. No, not that you wanted to die, but that you'd given up wanting to live. Those were different things, but I didn't know the difference then. Now I do. Now I wish I could go back and ask the right questions. Say the right thing about your elaborate collections.

*

Death, you can take me whenever you want, but let my dogs live, leggy and full of energy. You can take me dramatically or quietly but stop talking to my mother. She isn't ready. She's still waiting for my father's ghost to stand on the threshold, arms full of roses, the flower we're allergic to. For him to say, "I picked these for you."

Today in Signs

today I don't have much
to say walked to the field
listened to frogs rabbits
hurried everywhere away
the dead aren't coming back
but when we talk with them
they just might hear
I've stopped looking for signs
because they're everywhere
nothing isn't a sign
nothing is nothing which is itself
something: holding the space
between things so they stay
separately themselves
often I talk to my father
feel his ghost nearby
I tell my mother
she can haunt me anytime

Acknowledgments

Thanks to the following publications, where early versions of these poems first appeared:
"Overdue," *Foundry*
"Stray," *Healing Visions*, Matter Press
"Unexpected Side Effects of the Second Dose of the Moderna Vaccine,"
    "The Year I Stayed Inside," "1978," Black Lawrence Press blog

*

Thanks to my friends and family, especially Nichola Torbett, Meg Brown, Leslie Scott, Harvey Hawks, Jeanne Yeasting, and Debra Salazar.

Thanks to Diane Goettel and everyone at Black Lawrence Press for years of artistic curiosity and collaboration. Working with BLP is always a joy. You've made a home for my words for years now and I can't thank you enough.

Thanks to my colleagues and students at Western Washington University; and to Suzanne Paola, Bruce Beasley, Kiik Araki-Kawaguchi, Kelly Magee, Felicia Cosey, Amanda Hare, Rochelle Hurt, Taneum Bambrick, Wendy Fox, Robert Lashley, Alison Bruns, Jane Blunschi, Hillary Leftwich, Kelly Weber, chip phillips, and my poem-a-day friends for creating community.

Thanks to Todd Horton for the gorgeous cover art.

Special thanks to Clyde Petersen for everything.

This book is dedicated with love and gratitude to my mother, Gerry Guess.

Carol Guess is the author of numerous books of poetry and prose, including *Sleep Tight Satellite* and *Doll Studies: Forensics*. A frequent collaborator, she writes across genres and illuminates historically marginalized material. In 2014 she was awarded the Philolexian Award for Distinguished Literary Achievement by Columbia University. She is Professor of English at Western Washington University, where she teaches Queer Literature and Creative Writing.